An Abyss of Stars

Susie McBeth

Owl Light Books

Published by Owl Light Books
www.susiemcbeth.net

ISBN: 9798389738676

To River and Indigo
with all my love and
to Rob, for always
making sure there is a
light at the end of the
dark.

Foreword

I have always loved poetry. When I was eleven years old, I entered a poetry contest where if you won, your poem would be included in a poetry anthology, an actual published book! And I was so excited that I could not stop thinking or talking about it for weeks. I must have written so many different drafts and then finally entered my single entry (no multiple entries were allowed), a poem about love and what the idea of love was to me. It got included, and even now, as silly as it is, it still fills my heart with joy that it was included.

Poems to me are like magical incantations; some are crafted in language dripping in frosting and twists and turns that dress the world with the fanciest of blankets, and some create images of devastation or looks into other times. Some woo, and some make you cry; some are dotted on the page in a manner of shapes making the reading a journey, and all are magic.

My poetry is not fancy. It is not gilded and moulded with gold leaf (I actually love poems like this too, but it is not me). My words are simple, personal and crafted with love. I have dug deep and shared some of my sweetest memories and some of my saddest thoughts and feelings, and this is a very personal collection.

An abyss of stars purposely jumps between childhood moments, random thoughts, memories and significant points of my life as an adult because life is messy. I tried to tap deep into the advice I have, over the years, been given or have learned for myself in some of my more difficult times. I have also explored my gratitude for this opportunity to live and experience the many wonders of this crazy planet we inhabit. Is there anything really more beautiful or mysterious than the ocean?

To me, we are all unreliable narrators as we have one scope to look through, and it is our own. I have tried to showcase this in the order of my poems and thoughts. When I look backwards or forwards, it feels the same as when I looked through a kaleidoscope as a child, where colours and shapes fall into place seemingly randomly, though when you look close enough, there is always beauty to be found. While it is not always obvious, there is a pattern, and as you turn and twist, it evolves.

We all have poetry inside of us, whether it is written down or not. Our feelings are a very big part of what makes us, us. So, with that, I leave you with my simple words and gigantic feelings.

This is my first poetry collection, and I hope that it makes a connection.

Contents

Feathers...1
Strength from the sky...2
A new day..3
A history of beach pebbles...4
Broken biscuit breakfast..5
Lighting a spark...6
Get out the flashlights..7
The conversation was not ready to end....................8
A rose's protection..9
Painting..10
A tale of a 90's teen...11
A wish...12
Changes..13
Autoimmune...14
Friendship...15
Stretch..16
The problem with fear..17
Strength from the ocean..18
Let's lie here..19
Revolution/Youth..20
Be yourself..21
Two thirds..22
Through the telescope...23
Winter city walks...24
Nectar for sweet...25
Falling in love...26
Overshare...27
The patient friend..28
It's okay..29
The door...30
Christmas play..31
An uninvited guest..32

Contents

The beginning..34
Collector..35
Wonder..36
Midsummer every night.......................................37
Starting something new......................................38
It is not for nothing.......................................39
Vulnerable to liars...40
Strength..41
Choices...42
Date night..43
Thinking about death..44
Childhood...45
Strength from the earth.....................................46
Age 15: My summer of love...................................47
Libraries...48
Halfway...49
Too hard to love..50
Connection..51
You...52
Fresh start...53
Champion..54
The strength of tears.......................................55
I should have said no.......................................56
Lazy morning..57
Why forgiveness...58
Feelings..59
The end...60
The temporary nature of liars...............................61
My life as a dreamer..62
Hidden..63
The girl in the cupboard....................................64

Contents

An attempt at Spring...65
Restless thoughts...66
The ocean...67
Give it some time...68
My best friend Fudge..69
Act of betrayal...70
Oh, Christmas tree..71
It's not about me (well, it shouldn't be)...........................72
There is no lifeboat..73
Goodbye...74
A chant for survival..75
Ice storm...76
The power of dreaming...77
A spell of intent...78

Acknowledgements..81
Doll Parts (Bonus Short Story)......................................83
About the Author..89

Feathers

I wish I could be a crow.
Eyes dark, blinking with knowledge
A harbinger to some
A creature of magic to others
An omen
Or maybe a sign?
Sitting from an old gate post.
Watching the grass sway and the humans walk by.
Waiting for the call of my brothers and sisters
The feeling of flight
The excitement and leap from ground to air
Crowding the sky,
A murder.
Shifting on the wind, soaring, cawing
Feeling at one with myself and my family.
My feathers cutting through the chaos of life.

Strength from the sky

When I'm scared
I look up at the sky
And imagine the stars looking down
I feel the air on my face
And the sheer possibility of wonder
Everywhere

And for a moment, I feel my chest loosen
And I can breathe again.

A new day

The bud inches out her petals
One by one
Stretching her face to the sun
Today she knows she will grow.

History of beach pebbles

The pebbles lie still on the beach
In frothy white blankets
that get ripped away
They shine
They glisten
They get removed;
from the edge of the ocean
They weather,
They age
Their tales etched in lines on a surface no longer smooth
They get collected
In pockets,
On shelves
Where they are forgotten.

Broken biscuit breakfast

The TV is on a low hum
my sisters and I
sit close to hear
nightgowns on
letting the joy
of Saturday morning cartoons
wash over us in glows of orange and blues.
Crumbs of broken biscuits
line our mouths
marking the moment.
A once-in-a-month treat
while the lions sleep in.

Lighting a Spark

I found my hope in books.
Portals to worlds where adventure reigned
and love flowered in abundance.
The crackle and flame of punishment
burning the page did nothing to stall the feeling.
For the words had transferred
and were etched deep inside.
Writing their map of escape.
Always close, under my skin.
No matter how far the darkness spread,
The spark was lit, and the journey had begun.

Get out the flashlights

There is a hesitation
just before I run my fingers and palms
Under my arms
And feel my breasts
On a hunt for lumps
and bumps or mysteries
That will change my life forever.
I hold my breath
Unable to relax while I investigate
Every centimetre.
Thinking of women and men
Some who I know,
Like dear Polly,
and others I don't.
Whose bodies were invaded by cells
intent on harm.
There is no bravery
Only fear.
I don't want to get sick
But it is better to know,
so, each week
I ready my fingers
And search.

The conversation was not ready to end.

Even though you are gone
I still check your social media
All the time.
I don't know what I'm expecting
Your Twitter is frozen
It feels like a conversation stopped
Abrupt.
Mid-pause.
Now silent,
And the silence is the worst.

A rose's protection

The thorn is special
It protects the beauty
So the petals can grow lush
And it protects the bud
When the beauty has wilted
Ready for rebirth.

Painting

Paint stains my fingers.
The traces of a painting
Carried away from the canvas
I know it will wash off
But even though it will soon be gone
I love that it becomes a piece of me,
It doesn't replace the piece
I gave to the canvas
But it is a piece full of comfort
that will live on forever
Even after the acrylic fades
And washes down the drain.

A tale of a 90s teen

Red phone boxes with rusting metal and cold foggy glass
A shelter for tears
A place for small coins
that race through the slots never quite sticking.
A haven for secrets, dial tones, slammed handsets
And also excitement, when
Finally!
The right voice met you on the line.

A wish

I want to see with eyes
that don't only see mirrors
To be able to look deep
Beyond.

Changes

I have a poem that someone wrote for me when I was travelling.

He wrote it on a page of my journal, and when I got home, I ripped out the page and framed it. Year after year, it gets more faded, and I know that soon it will disappear forever. When it is gone, it will be like it never existed in the first place.

This is how I feel about myself. The more I change as a person, the further away I am from whom I used to be.

Autoimmune

It's a blue day
Cerulean washes
Stain the skyline
Hiding the flashes of red
And the dashes of yellow
That light up my body.
Fusing my veins with an ache
That doesn't disappear.
When asked, I say I'm fine
That's what I always say
While crossing my fingers
And hoping that the reds and yellows
Stay contained.

Friendship

There is a vibration in the earth

When we are close:
Hand to hand
In a hug
Online, blue-lit glowing, connected by screens
Or, just a voice in my head
Disconnected by years but not by heart

I can feel it.

Stretch

My body is a map
Little silver lines mark tales
Known and unknown
They spread across every curve
Rooted deep
Whispering my history
A marker of twins
A reminder of cake and tears
Happy and sad.

The problem with fear

I met you with 13-year-old eyes and a wary heart
A dream hidden beneath my tear-soaked pillowcase
It was weird to me that you were a reality.
You talked of love and excuses; a childhood paid in
photographs
But I couldn't hear you
My mind cloudy, and my ears closed.
When you reached for me,
I felt sick with fear and dizzy with hope
You touched my face, and I felt sure you could feel the
coldness lurking beneath the surface.
The heat of longing, struggling to break free of the ice.
I wanted to know you, to hug you, to love you.
I wanted to need you.
I wanted to escape and live in the fairy tale that I had created
in my head.
The one with the picket fence and daddy-daughter dance
The one where I wasn't by myself, wondering if you loved
me
The one that didn't include the bottle of demons that was
your closest friend
And now I am alone again.
All I have left is a ragged wallet full of yellow-eared pictures
of a six-year-old me,
And a brief memory,
Where your David Bowie eyes asked for love
And I was too scared to give it.

Strength from the ocean

I pull strength from the ocean
Her waves lift me up
Keeping me afloat
Moulding to my body, no matter my shape
I am just a tiny spec in her arms
But she lets me know
I'm an integral part

Let's lie here

Soft under sheets of white
Hiding from the sunlight
Warming our bodies with hands and mouths
Whispering, kissing, dreaming
The only reality is the one we have created.

Revolution/Youth

Seeds of revolution scatter
Ready to grow
Change is inevitable
And even though you take away
Heat, stability, education and safety
The seeds are strong
They will bud and flourish
It won't be a wasteland forever.

Be yourself

Take your time
Find out what it is that
You want
You need
You love
You dislike
And live your truth.

Two thirds

On the day you were born
My heart split into three
One part for Indigo
One for River
And one for me.
At first, I thought my heart was much smaller
As I'd given two-thirds away
But when you both smiled
Or sighed
Or cried
And as you grew
And talked
And thought
I knew
That my heart was not small
Not tiny
Or empty
It was bigger
It was heavier
And lighter
And stronger
And while it was a third
Of its original size
It beat so hard
Like all the wings in the sky
And it would never ever
Not feel full

Through the telescope

I am a small spec
In an abyss of stars.
It's not oblivion
It is a state of intention
In a universe so vast.
I'm grateful to take up
my tiny bit of space
And live.

Winter city walks

Slush drenched streets
Broken skin from slipping
Noise from traffic
Overwhelming at every decibel
An unexpected saviour:
Finding comfort in headphones
Covering me in a bubble of calm
Protecting me from the clamour
A safe place in a storm.

Nectar for sweet

I speak in nectar and honey
With my words, I caress
A delectable delight of want
A passion that is only brighter in the dark

My tongue trails honey down your spine, your jaw, your
belly
And leaves whispers of desire
Etched deeply
Magnetic to the fingertips

Passion curls deep within the darkest depths
The licks of flames are what bring in the light
The heady scent of a secret

Falling in love

I soared
Arms spread out wide
Running so fast
Down a hill
Without a stumble
Feeling the air carry me
As I raced through the cobwebs
Feeling my heart grow fuller

On this day
I fell in love with the wind.

Overshare

I want to tell you everything.
Spill my guts like pomegranate seeds
Pepper you with white-hot truths
That burn and sting with their grace.
Instead, I am silent.

The patient friend

The moon has a quiet courage.
It shines no matter its cycle.
It pulls on the tides
Cajoling them like unruly tweens unwilling to go to bed
It spins
It stays,
It stays, and it waits
It is a constant calm, a friend
Even when we worship the sun.

It's okay

It's ok not to be ok.
But recognise the need to breathe.
Take a moment and feel all that you need to feel
The prickles wrapping tight around your pulsing heart
The sting that brings tears with a sharpness
And the ache of the weight of the thorns.
Exhale slowly and let it all go
And know that no matter how hard it gets
That it's ok not to be ok
But you will be ok.
And the weight of the sadness will make room for the
sweetness of happiness once again.

The door

The light flickered in and out.
The wall, cold against my back, holds me up.
The door locked and closed.
Keeping me safe from the strangers in this house.
This hostel.
This place of in-between.
But the door can't stop this moment.
It can't stop the end of childhood.
Adulthood was not what I expected.

Christmas play

The chatter of the crowd
So loud
The rustle of coats
and programs
Thrumming to the beat
of chairs squeaking
Trying to all fit
The quiet giggle and hum
of the children backstage
Me, alone
In a crowded hall
Staring down at my phone
While all the other parents
group up
For a moment,
it feels like high school
But my awkwardness doesn't matter
only the look on their faces
When the play begins
and my children see me
Clapping.

An uninvited guest

Grief moved in with me one day
An uninvited guest.
Unwilling to leave or pay rent
Content to take my energy
Determined to bleed my strength.

While covering me in blankets
of dry-heaving sobs and unanswered questions.
Feeling crowded and empty
Anger decided to join the party.

Hiding at the back of every cupboard
Shadowing my every move
Making themselves known chaotically
Slowly I withdrew.

The world on the outside too sharp in focus
The world inside crowded and without meaning
Bones aching from the effort of existing.

Every minute a sprint
Each second an intense strategy to appear normal.

Always carrying an unbearable weight.

Anger's stay ended up being short
After carving permanent marks in the furniture
They took their leave.
Leaving Grief and I in an uneasy truce.

There was more space without anger.
And along with the wounds under my fingernails and skin
Anger had left me a gift.
A box unwrapped, full of energy and need
A spark without the vitriol
A yearning to feel alive.

Grief still took up room but stayed in the background
Quiet but still there, lingering
While slowly, I learned how to live again.

The light crept in through the windows
And the world outside beckoned me to explore

And even though I was scared, Grief encouraged me to try.
In the end, my uninvited guest became my friend.

The beginning

We bare our souls
In the attempt of friendship.
It is a leap of faith
In trust.

Collector

You speak pretty words
And like a magpie
I scoop them up
Eager for more
They glint with silver
Precious to the touch
But when I look closer
the truth is hidden in foil.

Wonder

There is wonder in every facet of life
In every moment, from the stark beauty of a tear
To the dew clinging to a blade of grass
Details that are easy to miss
But if seen, will carve a space in your heart
Filling it with energy and light.

Midsummer every night

Each night Puck visits
and whispers mischief
Into the ears of those willing to listen.
His loving chaos
wraps around sleeping bodies
Soft like a sheet,
cool as a spring dew,
vibrating into waking life.

Starting something new

There is a crunch to winter
A crispness to autumn
A sheen to summer
But spring manages to be all of those things all at once.
It is the season of birth.
Of rain kissing the ground and the sun drying it out.
It is a time of renewal
A whisper of hope
A time for making plans.

It is not for nothing

If a flower wilts
It is not for nothing.
It lived vibrantly with every ounce of its being
Its memory etched into nature,
the falling petals, one with the earth engrained forever.

Vulnerable to liars

My eyes are glazed with stars.
My vision blurred by dust and noise.
My sight lost in the beauty.
Easily swayed by pretty words.
Felt deep
Accepted because hope lines my stomach.

Strength

Strength sings in your blood
It shows up in the grace of tears
The acceptance that something you want
Can't be yours
Waking up every day and choosing to live
Even when it's hard
It shines in your eyes
When you determine to find joy
In the every day
And share gratitude.
It is a lion's roar that bubbles your soul
And you are always stronger than you know.

Choices

It is so easy to say nothing
To cast your eyes down to the floor
And hope you disappear.
But when you find your voice,
Even though it can feel like
You are pushing through a crowd
Where you're knee-high and the masses
Are towering over you
The world shifts.
The feeling of unease starts to dissipate.
Your eyes see everything
Not just the granite beneath your feet.
And you may be shaking with nerves,
But those nerves are a marker
Of bravery.

Date night

I will wait for you
At the end of the world.
We will catch stars
And carve out something new
Because with you
There is no end.

Thinking about death

Sometimes I lie here
and think about death.
What happens next?
Is it just blank?
A state of nothing.
Forever darkness where we cease to be?
Or is it something else?
A release of energy,
a return to life inside another body,
Heaven, hell, or just somewhere else?
Maybe a different universe or reality?
Do we become ghosts?
Haunting in crowded spaces,
longing for the lives we lost.
Or do we just wander the earth,
spectres not happy or sad,
just there in new forms?
The thoughts overwhelm me.
There are so many layers and possibilities
It's paralyzing.
I wish we knew.
I'm scared
Yet, I still want to know what comes next.

Childhood

Under the covers
A world lit only by plastic and glass
Holding my breath
I try to silence the page before the creak on the stairs.
Muffling the light with a pillow
Still like a statue waiting for you to pass.

Strength from the earth

I draw strength from the earth
I feel the growth beneath the soil
Reaching out to all corners
and beyond
The shoots of green and pops of colour
Fill me with joy
They are a buoy
That lift me through the intermittent darkness

Age 15: My summer of love

We lay
Whispering
Giggling
Touching
Kissing
Hidden by the corn.
My heart felt light
While my butterflies fluttered
And you,
you looked at me
And I felt seen.

Libraries

There is a certain smell to libraries.
A kind of yellowing must
mixed
with the lingering contrived
sweetness of furniture polish.
Dusty old books and silence
line the shelves
drowning out the rustling of pages
and thoughts spiralling
in and out of inspiration and sleep.
I love it.

Halfway

The wind curls around the words
Whistling through the blades of grass
That crush underfoot with a sigh
The soles of my feet blister when I'm only halfway there
No matter how much time passes
It is always halfway
The wind curls around the words
And only the grass can hear them.

Too hard to love

When you tell someone, they are too hard to love, they
believe you.

Long after lights out, my eyes still swollen from crying
I hold my breath and pressed my face into my pillow,
Pretending to sleep.

Your whisper of sorry, a hint at guilt as always gave me
hope.
Maybe tomorrow would be better?

My head felt bruised from the roots.
An invisible mark to everyone but me.

Connection

I am a tiny part of the cosmos
Essential, detailed, a universe contained within
Just like you.
And we,
We are connected by stardust.

You

Your scent sticks to me
Conjuring movie reels that play beneath closed eyes
You are cinematic
every detail etched in the brightest colours
I feel overwhelmed by you
Even alone, I'm surrounded by you.
Your touch
Your hands moving under my shirt, scraping my back
The need
Your mouth
Soft and hard
Your tongue, pushing me deeper
I know I should pull away
Yet I don't.

Fresh start

The dawn is quiet
The early morning sun
Reaches down and blesses my face
Eyes closed,
forehead raised to the sky
Waiting for the birds to sing
Feeling deep in the moment
The frost-tipped air nibbling at my skin
On the precipice of something wonderful
A new day,
A new start
A heart brimming over with gratitude.

Champion

Fierce
Red fired heart
You race around with vim
And slay dragons
I watch you in awe.

The strength of tears

I cry so much.
Alice's pool of tears
Is a puddle compared
to the tsunami
That flows from me
Trails of salt streak my face
And sting my eyes
Happy or sad
Angry or frustrated
The tears are a reminder.
Of the depth of feeling
It all matters
And I am stronger for it.

I should have said no

Resentment strangles my thoughts
Though my tongue is silent.
I hate that I end up having to go against
My very being because I was the only choice left.
I should have said no.
You should have done something so that this was not even a
thing.
I resent myself just as much
as I resent you for making me do it.
And now resentment is wrapped around my insides,
Vines holding me tight
And all I want to do is sleep.

Lazy morning

I hide
Under the covers
It's warm
And so cosy.
Sheets soft against my skin
Hiding from the light
Taking a pause
in the space between morning and more.
A cocoon of dreams
And possibility
Delaying the day.

Why forgiveness

Should you always forgive?
Does it help you move past the ghosts?
The weight of stress in your veins
The echoes that chase your steps
Does it bring you peace?
I'm not sure.
Even if I wanted to forgive,
I'm not sure I can.
And right now, blood may be thicker than water
But that just means you are harder to wash away.
It doesn't mean that I can't,
and it doesn't mean that I won't.

Feelings

When I was young
I wore my heart on my sleeve
And felt everything so deeply
I lived in a place of need.
With the years passing
I thought I'd become hollow
I'd feel less of the joy
And less of the sorrow.
But I realise that I feel
just as much, if not more
Though I hide it so well
Locked away deep in my core
Now when I cry
My nerves are electric
From elbow to fingers
They throb unrestricted
My chest opens wide
and the cavern I thought empty
Is full to the brim
My feelings are plenty.

The end

I don't hate or resent you
There is no contempt
But then there is no love either

The temporary nature of liars

Lies wrap you in wisps of silk
Adjusting to every shape and occasion
A fit perfect in feel but easily torn.

My life as a dreamer

Vivid dreams
Blur the lines
Softening the edges
Bleeding through
Seeping into the waking life
Until I'm not sure what is real.

Hidden

You can hide so much behind a smile
It is terrifying the depth of suffering
That is hidden behind upturned lips
And happy words.

The girl in the cupboard

I locked you away
Small and scared
Your heart clutched tight,
Close to your chest.
I heard your cries
Your pleas
To come out and play,
To come out and feel,
And I shushed you aside.
You were drowned out
by the voices of others
Their needs became my needs,
And the space for you grew even smaller.
I want to let you out
I want my heart back in my chest
And you, the little me
Who is scared and sad
I want us to reunite.
I believe one day, we can feel complete.
I just need some space
I just need to look after us.

An attempt at Spring

I can hear the daffodils.
Their green shoots trying to break through the
Semi-frozen soil
While the custard glazed sun
flickers through the skeletons of trees
whispering to all who will listen
Grow, grow, grow.

Restless thoughts

Time does not know me.
But it dictates my being.
It is up to me to fill any holes.
Why, when in pain, does the world seem to stand still?
I ache
The passion I feel overwhelmes
Sadness controls who I am
I long for the interludes of happiness
Is anyone ever complete?
Does anyone, if they are complete, stay complete?

The ocean

My sadness is a weight spreading out from my belly across
all my limbs.
Its tendrils wrap around my muscles, binding me tightly
There is a pain, but it is blurry and undefined. When I feel
like this, the world turns to water.
The cold and dark of the deep swallow me up.
I pierce the surface now and then, but there is no air.

Give it some time

When I see snow crunched down
Smothered to ice
It reminds me
That not all transformations
Are pretty.
Slowly the weight of the frozen slush
holding the grass in place
Melts
Seeping back into the earth
Leaving a freshness
That was forgotten
And I realise that
The transformation is
Not always finished
When you think it is.
And some things are worth the wait.

My best friend Fudge

She barks
She jumps
She zooms
She takes over my space on the bed
She runs from her harness while
grumbling when I don't get her ready
for her walk fast enough
And she fills me with so much delight.
Her little face
Her brown eyes that sparkle with curiosity
Her attempts to jump to help me lift her up
Her abundance of magic and excitement
She is the friend I never knew I wanted
And my favourite one to walk with.

Act of betrayal

Attack!
All armies mobilise.
An intruder is attacking us
We must defeat it!
White cells shed
In a dead of dark green
Flowing and flowing.
Attack!
But what are you attacking?
We are attacking ourselves.
Autoimmune,
An act of betrayal.

Oh, Christmas tree

My story becomes your story
Told in baubles and glitter
An eclectic mix of ornaments
That carefully adorns you.
Memories flow with each nudge onto the branch
Each one placed with absolute care.
The tinsel smells of the past
a moment that was shared.
A glimmer of happiness
in a childhood mostly bare.
The twinkly lights that dress you glow.
Filling my heart with joy.

It's not about me (well, it shouldn't be)

I feel like I'm surrounded by death
Cancer, COVID, Suicide
People on the verge
The tipping point of illness
or desperation,
And I feel helpless.
I feel
I FEEL.
I'm mad at myself for making it about how **I feel**.
I'm dreaming about it,
Writing birthday cards in nightmares
For the twins, for the years ahead.
Making peace while realising
there is no peace to be found.
My stomach is squirming,
and I feel the whispers
Coming at me from all sides
Claustrophobic to the max
I just want it to stop.

There is no lifeboat

"I prefer when you smile
Your energy is better."
"I know," I said
Trying to hide the fact
That I was drowning.

Goodbye

I feel as if my eyes are
Crusted constantly in salt
My face streaked with tears
My chest hurts when I sob.
A velvet crush of laughter
and a warmth that drew us in
You were soft with a side of vulnerable
A creative with so much vim
I can't pretend to understand
I hope you are at peace
I wish you were still here, my friend
And I know that feeling won't cease

A chant for survival

I am strong and resilient
I am full of gratitude and love
I am strong and resilient
I am full of gratitude and love

*Repeat until you believe it.

Ice storm

The quiet of the storm
Is interrupted by fairy bells
Ice meeting ice
In a symphony
Searing through the silence
In a wave of blue
The frozen grass
Listens
Alert, standing to attention
In awe of the beauty of winter
Lakes lay frozen and perfectly in place
While swirling in turmoil beneath the surface
Flowers face the ground
Petals hardened in the bud
Longing for the warmth of the sun
And the feel of the supple earth
Waiting for the treacherous
Cold
To end

The power of dreaming

When you dream, you can do anything
When you wake, you can make your dreams happen.
So now I dream hard and live with purpose.

A spell of intent

Words are magic, so speak with intention.

Acknowledgements

This poetry collection has been pieced together from scraps of time that I have managed to eke out wherever I can.

Some of these poems I have been sitting on for a long time, and some recently finessed into something consumable. It has been a labour of love and emotion where I have had some essential time to get to know myself and how I am feeling and share some of that with you, the person reading this. So, with that said; hopefully, at least some of it resonated and made sense.

First of all, I want to thank Rob for helping me manage to get some me time so that I could write, and also, I want to thank my friends, Sharon, Carly, Erika, Iris and Cecilia and my sister Helen, for the encouragement and for giving me the pat on the back needed so I could strengthen my resolve to be brave and put myself out there.

I want to thank Cecilia again as not only was she cheering me on, but she also proofread this little book – so, thanks muchly for that.

And best and most of all, thank you to you! I appreciate you reading this. It is always so amazing to me when someone takes time out of their life and spends some of it on something I created.

P.S. Read on for a bonus short story.

Story time

I love to write, whether it be poems, short stories, novels or my journal. I am constantly scribbling away. So, as a bonus, I have included a dark and twisty short story called Doll Parts. It is a little different in tone – but I think it is always nice to include a little something extra, and this time, it is this! I hope you enjoy it.

Doll Parts

You had to be careful of your feet; the flats were one part marsh, one part grass and the rest mud and stone. There was nothing flat about them which made the name of the grasslands that backed onto the end of our street pretty strange.

The grass, yellowed-green and long, covered the booby traps that lay in wait for our teenage feet, ready to trap or trip us. Jeremy Lish broke his ankle, tripping over a molehill, and I heard it took over four hours before anyone found him. We weren't supposed to go there, but everybody did. We didn't tell our parents; we left them lost in their cocktails and gossip while we lived real life.

Even the chain link fence the council installed to block off access didn't stop us. Within a month, there was a hole big enough to squeeze through. Our clothes, the victim of consequence, bearing the brunt in ripped seams and holes. We weren't worried about toxic waste; we were pretty sure all the talk about contamination was grade-A adult bullshit designed to scare us into playing by the rules.

The factory that stood at the end of the flats had been out of business for decades. Its imposing chimneys, scorched black, sat silently amongst the concrete grey of the uniform buildings stacked poorly like forgotten LEGO bricks. This was our place.

At night we would light it with torches. Talking loudly, singing crappy versions of bad pop songs. Poking fun at each other while getting stoned and drinking illicitly brought cans of Special Brew that somehow always tasted stale. In the summer, we would climb up and stretch out on the flat roof of the dilapidated office building, feeling the sun lick our faces while we talked about who was supposedly dating who and got lost in daydreams.

During school holidays, the factory became the centre of my day. Sadie and I would usually run through the flats together, our pockets stuffed with food and our heads full of excitement. We would whittle away the days, sometimes doing homework, other times exploring the grounds. Joking that one day we would run away and live here together permanently, away from the rules and restrictions.

Alex and Josh would meet us for a few hours here and there, but mostly we were left to ourselves during the week. Other people's parents wanted to know where they were. Our freedom was freely given through wilful ignorance and the bliss of 'don't ask, don't tell.' At home, we lived like ghosts. Melting into the walls, trying our best not to be noticed. No eye contact, the sting of love felt in the bite of a belt.

Sadie would worry that we would get caught, and a part of me wished we would. Maybe one day, the consequence would be the means of our escape. This was not ever to be.

It was a Sunday in Autumn when our visits to the factory came to an end. My lungs felt like they were bursting, my heart slammed against my chest, and the chill of the wind burned red into my cheeks. Sadie and Alex were already at the factory; their playground teases had blossomed into full-on teenage love. They had it bad.

Mooney eyes, the groping of body parts and the never-ending commentary of "do you think he likes me, you know, like, really likes me?"

Sadie would lie in her bunk and whisper to me all night about how perfect he was, seemingly forgetting that I had known him just as long as she – and that he still seemed to me, to be a slightly spotty boy with a pretty good sense of humour. The Adonis she painted didn't really match up to what I was seeing. I didn't care; I was happy she was happy. I gladly covered for the two of them. Whispered details of non-existent school projects in mum's ear, so they could spend long afternoons holed up together at the factory in private, completely absorbed in their love bubble.

This time though, when I ran to meet them, there was an eerie silence. My breathing as I tried to catch my breath sounded harsh and too loud, almost overwhelming. My legs, wobbly from my ever-unsteady run across the flats, were jelly-like and uncooperative.

I ran my thumb and forefinger along the rim of my coat, a nervous habit I had been cultivating since birth. Something was not right. There was no birdsong. The leaves scattered across the ground were silent, and Sadie and Alex were as still as statues.

Their hands were clasped together so tightly that even from a couple of feet away, I could see their knuckles shine white, their backs ridged, and their muscles taut. As I walked closer, I noticed a smell. It reminded me of rotten leaves and roadkill, and the closer I got to Sadie and Alex, the worse it was. I felt sick. I wanted to speak, but my voice left me. No words could cut through the tension.

I glanced over at Sadie. She was blotchy and red and had silent tears streaming down her face, and Alex looked green. It was only after watching them that I steeled myself to look at what they were.

Seconds passed and time stretched. My stomach lurched. Swallowing back the vomit that threatened to showcase my lunch, I looked at the arm that was reaching out to us from underneath the brambles. Pale like porcelain and scratched with what looked like tear stains but were a dark, gritty brown that reached from the elbow to the wrist. Bent at a weird angle and ever so still, it looked so foreign against the backdrop of the concrete grey and green.

The nail polish was a deep pink and chipped in the way that only girls who pick off their nail varnish know. There was something elegant and terrible about it, and I felt frozen. An image of one of Nanna Gotty's old dolls kept flashing before my eyes. Solid yet delicate, made of old china and horror-film creepy. Every time we stayed at her house, I would feel the doll eyes watching me from the shelf above my bed until I screwed up my courage, got up and turned them around to face the wall. Slowly I noticed a fiery tangle of red slightly further up. The brightness in complete contrast to the green and black of the bush. The grey eyes stared out at me, blank and empty, asking me a question I could never know the answer to.

When sound returned, all I could hear was heavy breathing interspersed with sobs and retching. Falling onto my knees, scuffing them on the stones, I didn't even feel the blood as it ran down my legs and into the dirt. The cries were my own, and as my stomach emptied itself on the ground around me, I didn't even notice that Sadie and Alex had left.

I was alone with her. Her blank eyes watched me as I unsuccessfully tried to bite back the bile. I tried to speak, but only animal-like cries would come out.

Sadie sat across from me at dinner in her usual seat. Shaking her head, intonating that I needed to stay silent, so I did. I couldn't eat, and after three hours of sitting at the table in silence with a stone-cold plate of food, my mum gave up and sent me to my room.

When I finally returned to the factory, there was no sign of her. The smell had gone, the birds had returned, and everything seemed normal – even though I knew nothing would ever be the same again. That was the last time, and I know I will never go back.

Thanks for reading!

About the Author

Susie McBeth is a first-time poet living on the Wirral in the UK. An Abyss of Stars is her first poetry collection.

She has previously published a book of short stories called the Heart Exchange: And 11 other stories and a short humorous book designed to be read in a coffee break called How to Become a Supervillain in 10 Easy Steps.

When not writing, you can find her making cute and messy art, marketing video games (it's her job!), walking with her dog Fudge and spending time with her family. Susie is also an avid tea drinker and she one-day dreams of designing her own special blend!

Find more of her work:
susiemcbeth.net
@susiemcbeth (on Twitter and Instagram)

Other Works by Susie McBeth

The Heart Exchange: And 11 Other Stories

How to Become a Supervillain in 10 Easy Steps

Available on Amazon.

Coming 2023: Interlude

Image plates

1.   An Abyss of Stars
2.   Lost key
3.   Growing
4.   The Sky Above
5.   Mother Earth

All drawn by Susie McBeth.

Printed in Great Britain
by Amazon